Blue in the Red House

Sarah Madden

Obiter
Publishing

Published by Obiter Publishing
PO Box 5133
Braddon ACT 2612
info@obiterpublishing.com.au
www.obiterpublishing.com.au

ISBN-13: 978-0-6481742-3-3

NATIONAL LIBRARY OF AUSTRALIA
A catalogue record for this book is available from the National Library of Australia

Cover design by Nadia Ingrid
© Nadia Ingrid 2018
Design by Aidan Delaney
Printed by Ingram Spark

In the beginning...

It took a very long time to find a doctor who would see me on the matter; the matter being, of course, the putting out of my eyes.

I had seen enough, and I wasn't scared of the dark or anything, not anymore. I was prepared to take in nothing else over the course of my remaining days. I felt good about never seeing my woes, not ever again. There were already so many things travelling in my head, I really didn't think I needed to add to it. I'd made a lot of calls to a lot of clinics, making sure to practice using the voice-dial feature of my smarter-than-me phone to do so. I imagined clever tech would be my lifeline once the lights were out.

It was a bright day, all vibrant, blue-green, smug with natural wonder. It was too bright for me, and I wore three pairs of sunglasses to combat the thing – two normal pairs, one slightly larger than the other and stacked, then wedged in place with the third, those 'over glasses' that elderly women wear on top of their proper glasses. They look like extras from an old sci-fi film when they wear them. I imagined that I did too, especially as the request I was to make of the doctor was well before its time and I was boldly going something someone somewhere, y'know.

Settling into the dusty, 1970s-style chair in the doctor's room, I silently bade farewell to the eye chart on the wall, the scales, the healthy eating leaflets and the diabetes info-sheets. I bade them farewell as if the joke was on them. The doctor sat too, crossed his legs, and picked up something I couldn't quite make out from the table, a long blur with a nib. He had been the only medico that had agreed to see me.

"What can I help you with today, Ms. De Beer?"

"I would like to have my eyes removed. I've really thought about it a lot, and I'm just so sick of seeing everything. I think I'd be less sad and lonely if I didn't see what I was missing, and I'm really just ready to be in the dark."

"I see," he said, trying not to chuckle at his own little joke.

It wasn't very funny. I crossed my arms and decided that this person was unlikely to help me. He was the same as the rest – dismissive, amused, uncomprehending.

He asked me what I would like to replace my eyes with, if they were to be removed. I suggested pebbles, or coins, or marbles, or some kind of unremarkable sphere that wouldn't catch the light.

"I'd like to ask you some questions before we decide which path to tread," he said, picking up a book in which to scribble notes.

When he said 'some', he really meant 'loads of', and I was becoming impatient.

Where do you live?
Can you follow a map?
What is your middle name?
Do you ever suffer from chest pain?
How many fingers am I holding up?
What colour is an apple?

The scratch of the nib grated at my ears and I was about to pop with frustration when he stopped. He held up the notebook.

"Can you please read to me the words on this page?"

I looked at the notebook, but the page was bare.

"This is ridiculous, there's nothing on that page!"

The doctor swung around in his chair and made a few notes on his laptop. He slowly swung back, and asked me another, even stranger question.

"Can you name anything that is red?"

I could not name anything that was red. I tried to deflect the question with some philosophical hoo-ha about colour being perception, and perception being unreliable, but he wasn't having it.

"Can you see the puddle at your feet, Ms. De Beer?"

Looking at my feet, what I saw was the absence of a visible puddle of anything at all. I decided that this doctor was due some long-service leave. I was about to calmly make my excuses and retreat to the waiting room to make an appointment with a less discouraging practitioner when he got to the crux of it.

"I mean, I'm just surprised it's your eyes you're worried about, when the real issue is that your heart is bleeding almost non-stop.

"There is an enormous puddle of heart-blood under your chair, in the reception area, the waiting room, and a trail that leads all the way back to your little brick house at 37 Stanley Street. I know, because I sent Dr. Black to follow the bloodlines, and she double-checked your address and your usual haunts. There are old, dried trails from your front door that lead to the corner store, the booze shop, the library. I say 'haunts', but you're not dead as yet…"

"There must be some mistake, I would have seen that."

"Did you see my notes, the ones I made in red pen?"

I had not seen the notes, only the too-bright paper and the straight blue lines where the words were supposed to be. I had assumed he was making some absurd point.

Apparently, I had been crisscrossing the neighbourhood with these 'blood lines', mapping out my days and my travels for everyone to see but me. I did not know what red was. I wasn't seeing too much, I was not seeing enough. There were heartfelt gridlines that I followed without fail, and I had been unable to plot them or follow their predictable hope, but my heart's spectre had picked up the breadcrumb trail.

I slumped back in the chair, the one that I could only imagine was no longer brown, but red with my inability to see, and I felt soggy, soaked to the bone.

"I'm going to prescribe a course of red things to get you back in balance. Rare steak, raspberry soda, cherries, buy a pair of red shoes, watch a sunset for goodness sake – if you can see orange you'll know it's starting to work. Get some red thread and stitch up your thoughts. Cut yourself and see the result. Try to be more red and you'll see it."

I wondered if this was why the blooms on my rose-bushes never appeared. The buds were there, little green tents containing flowery things to come, but when they opened they were like gnarled hands grasping for petals that had floated away. I could smell them, but they never seemed to be there. Similarly, the oranges on the tree in my backyard always seemed so yellow that I avoided them for fear of being tricked by lemons.

That night I watched the sun go down. It only got halfway to the horizon before it faded to my view, and I supposed that was where it turned red. There was still the light though, and as I clicked the heels of my shoes together, the red ones that I could not see, I wondered what would happen if I painted it all 'red'.

Chapter One

Although she had half-heartedly feasted on strawberries and the rarest of lamb the previous evening, the day dawned blue-green as it had for all the days before.

It had been difficult to make out what was on her plate, the morsels were almost invisible save for blurred outlines, so she'd had to grasp at smudges and put them in her mouth.

Ms. De Beer had never been one for 'giving it her best shot'. Nor was she keen on 'following her dreams'. A plate full of food that may or may not have been there was cause for irritation, for quiet explosions at how stupid it was, and how she was really eating nothing at all and should be locked up for agreeing to such utter nonsense, but not before the doctor was.

Still, the sky was reassuringly blegh, if too bright again, and that was something. There were birds in it too, which was nice. And everything seemed to be moving just a bit to the right, moving away from Ms. De Beer at a gentle speed. Not running away (that would be rude), but at least not sticking around to give her pause to ponder on things, and certainly not pointing a finger or trying to chat. Away was much more comfortable than to.

It was with that comforting thought that she decided to move away too. A walk would work off the curiously full feeling she'd had after eating all the blurry nothing the night before. So she set out, willfully ignoring the urge to find the trails the doctor had mentioned as if they were some kind of fact. A walk required either a dropping-of-everything and close-of-the-door, or an elaborate packing ritual that catered for every eventuality. Today was a packing day, and her bag was filled with: a book (Salman Rushdie if you please), a pen, a notebook, cigarettes, lighter, wallet, keys, wooly hat (just in case), toothbrush and toothpaste (also just in case), sunglasses x 3, and raspberry licorice (which would probably disappear when she opened the package).

Footpaths were solid and grey and THERE, and so she followed them. Ms. De Beer had also never been one for deviating from the path, and she followed it gravely, eyes down and watching her feet touch with each step, not looking for a view so much as evidence of movement. She was moving, and it was the way things worked, and she was doing it too. If she were to move, then she was doing the thing, the actual thing not the no-thing, and she didn't want to be a no-thing at all. She might be mad and unable to see red, but she could keep moving, fuck it, she could move away, and to, although to had started to seem like a bad idea.

Perhaps, if she were to keep moving, the red ghost of her heart wouldn't be able to keep up. She could follow her nose, and that heart-blood line would always be behind her – no need to see it if she wasn't going the same way. That was the plan – leave the red behind her, and walk towards the lack, the lack that didn't know it was a lack of anything. It just waited for her to pass by, and kept moving its own way, getting what it needed from the heart-blood as she went, and neither was any the wiser for the transaction.

Ms. De Beer had wandered much further than was advisable, and for most of the day without noticing the passage of time. She was tired, and there appeared to be nowhere else to go – there was a lake to the front of her, murky and almost purple, but it couldn't be purple because she couldn't see anything with the red, and purple was infused with the red. It was purple, and murky and it wobbled, gelatinous and just about ready to blacken for the day with the setting of the sun. Gelatinous things always gave Ms. De Beer the heebie-jeebies, with their promise of fluidity on the surface, yet anything but underneath. You could plunge your hand in quite easily, but unlike the real, flowing stuff, something would always stick on the way back out. To gel was to leave something of yourself on the thing you bumped into, and that was almost as rude as running away.

She probably should have gone home then. Right in that moment she could have turned on her heel and she still wouldn't have been following anything – she couldn't see her trails anyway. There was something troubling about the purple of the lake, though, and the idea that in turning she might see the lines, and hear the doctor's voice in her head again telling her that she was heartily bleeding to a slow, lonely death, and, well that would be a waste of a nice walk. Just a walk actually. It wasn't that nice.

Deciding to pause for a while to consider her options, Ms. De Beer planted herself on a park bench at the edge of the lake. It was quite a thing, the purple of it, an enormous watery bruise, with brown wooden buildings jutting out into the calm, as if the wound were healing and scabbing over as structure spread across its lines. There was a small jetty with a little boathouse attached, all run-down and just like one of those pictures from a self-help book that symbolise some kind of 'you can do anything' sentiment. A rickety boat, very unsafe looking really, bobbed at the side of the boathouse, silently begging to be used for some kind of strange adventure that you only read about in books written by people whose sight seems a bit skewed. It was all out of a book, in one way or another.

Ms. De Beer felt very skewed indeed, and so it was without surprise that she found herself peering over the edge of the jetty and down at the boat, checking it for obvious leaks or unwanted fellow passengers. It was dry, the wood glowing in that way that old wooden things often do – soft as a kitten's paw and almost as irresistible. Sitting, of course and all-of-a-sudden, on the simple bench in the boat, she wondered where the oars were, not so as to go anywhere you understand, but perhaps they might be required in an emergency.

No oars. Ah well; the tiny spark of adventure began to fade in her chest. But she was moving nonetheless. The boat was slipping silently through the big bruised lake without so much as asking if that was ok, and it was soothing despite the fact she hadn't asked for it. Ms. De Beer peered at the lake's surface as she passed – at each side of the boat there seemed a current, a liquid highway carrying it forward with such natural grace that she almost felt a traitor for wishing it had asked permission. The rest of the lake was too busy being glassily serene, perhaps nourishing the fish or being a proper eco-thingy, although it was holding the current steady in a straight line, its stillness part of the architecture of movement.

"How are we moving?" she asked the boat.

"I'm not sure on that," said the boat in reply. "The current knows, but it whispers so quietly I can never hear the explanation."

"Oh well, at least we are moving, that's something. Where are we going?"

The boat said nothing, and Ms. De Beer wondered if it had, in fact, spoken at all, or if the doctor had been on to something with his gentle insinuations that she was going a bit mad.

The sky had properly darkened now, and the only thing distinguishing the water from the rest of the earthly things around her was the occasional sparkle of light hitting the veins of the current. There were no more birds up there either, and she could only suppose they'd stopped moving somewhere, the silly, motionless creatures. They were asking for someone to come and ruffle their feathers, and that was the thing best avoided.

So many things so ill-defined, as blurry as her feasting-plate, and she really couldn't find a better word than 'thing' to describe any of them.

Birds: feathery things that flew in the sky, then foolishly stopped.

Boat: wooden thing with a low voice that rudely stopped talking in the middle of a conversation.

Lake: thing that should be blue, but was unsettlingly purple, and was moving and not.

Ms. De Beer: confused thing that would stop if she stopped.

Then she stopped.

The boat nudged into the opposite shore. Ms. De Beer had been unaware of the potential end of the boat trip, having been too busy watching the current moving and marvelling at how lovely it must be to just move all the time without a destination. But there had been a destination, and she had bumped into it, and now she was here and a little bit disappointed if she were to be honest.

"Could you please get out?" the boat asked quietly. "I must turn soon, and you seem the sort to try and triple back when only doubling is required. I can't afford to go off course."

Ms. De Beer clumsily disembarked, thinking of a well-constructed diatribe with which to tongue-lash the boat back to the boathouse, to give it something to think about when it came to manners, and whether or not boats should talk. Her foot fell into the edge of the current, and as she was almost sucked along in the boat's turning wake, she decided that regaining her balance might be more important than giving the transportation a lesson in common courtesy.

Stepping up from the shallows onto the murky edges of what, she decided, must be an island, she shook her feet to get the remaining lake off her trouser cuffs and shoes. She was soaked with purple, but the light was so dim that it didn't seem to matter, or it wouldn't until morning at least.

A light shone through the elbows of a particularly old and ugly tree, the kind of tree that only looks appealing in the glow of something else, and Ms. De Beer winced at its roots as if they were little, vengeful anchors. She passed it in a wide arc, moving towards the light, but with enough distance that the tree and its moveless nature couldn't tether her as well. She filed away her use of the word 'moveless' for later defense – you never knew who you would have to defend your language to, even one's own skeleton could start an argument about foundations, and that was nothing to go into unprepared.

Ms. De Beer watched her feet even more closely than usual as she walked, making sure to avoid any overly suspicious looking roots. As she scanned the night-slick ground she noticed a scattering of pebbles in her path, all soft with the light they reflected. They were very good at causing the light to 'away' instead of 'to', so she picked up a few in different sized pairs, thinking of how dazzlingly dull they would look in her eye-less sockets once she'd had the op and installed them in place of her sight.

As was the way with Ms. De Beer, there was a sudden bump and exhalation, and she had come to the end of the path, a stone step jutting into the path of her boots, inviting 'up' with its nowhere-but-up-ness, and a practical solution to the sudden lack of forwards.

"Oof. Watch it, sunshine. I'm a step, not a kicking bag!"

The step would have clapped a hand firmly over its mouth, had it a hand to do so with, and in the minute or two of silence that followed, while Ms. De Beer collected her shock and reworked it into a reaction, it quietly berated itself for having broken character yet again.

"There is absolutely nothing in this world that is called a kicking bag, and while I understand that I may have injured you, there's certainly no cause to make things up," Ms. De Beer replied, finally and firmly, before realising she was talking to something that was probably not talking to her really, not really at all, and that she had made up a word only moments ago, and that she really was probably mad.

Before the argument could descend further into philosophical matters, she stepped up. The step, having been slightly aggrieved but now pleased that he'd got one to go 'up' finally, said nothing. Ms. De Beer looked at the door in front of her, and wondered how on earth she'd managed to find herself somewhere that involved knocking on a strange door and hoping that someone might let her in. She did knock, however.

She knocked too loudly, because perhaps the occupant was out the back of the house, or maybe they had the telly on, or the radio, or maybe they were a bit deaf. It was better to be quite obviously there, rather than be the thing that a person isn't sure they heard. To be mistaken for a tree branch hitting the window, for a cat walking past the sensor light, for the creaking noises a house makes when it shifts in the night, that was the most lonely mistake for a living, breathing hermit to endure, for when a solitary person knocks, they have never meant it more.

Ms. De Beer meant it, although it meant a 'going through' rather than a coming in. Being told to come in always felt as if the corner of the world to which she had been granted entry was poised to swallow her, and that she wouldn't be able to get back to her 'usual' before she was digested and secreted as an agent of somewhere else and its need for sustenance. Or maybe she just didn't like the curve of someone else's sofa, or the carpet, or the curtains with the pastel patterns and dusty hems. There was no need to sneeze out the air of the parlour if you never ventured inside.

And there was most definitely someone in there; she knew there was. The air hummed, just as it does when there's a television on somewhere in the house – you can't hear it, but its being on crackles in the air. When there's a person in a place, the biology of it spreads its pollen in the dust motes that play in the light, and the tiny floating things that skip across the eyes when their focus goes wonky. If Ms. De Beer had cared to peer through the window, she would have seen the human pollen rising and blooming and falling-for-a-moment in the light of the house. She had not cared to, so she waited, and hoped there was a back door to this place.

The place, the house on the island in the lake, was hard to make out, at least its lines seemed hard to place among the trees and all the other nature that clung to its sides. She began to wonder if she'd knocked on a door-shaped tree, or had been following a firefly's light to a rather large spider-web, but then the door creaked and she was greeted by a reflection so accurate that she wished the boat had been there to exclaim to in her fright.

It appeared she had knocked at her own door, and she had opened that door to herself, and was about to usher herself in.

"The boat never told me I was already here."

"It didn't tell me I was coming, either," she said to herself from the mouth of the other herself.

"I am Ms. De Beer."

"Yes, me too," she said to herself.

Chapter Two

"Well that's not going to work," the newest arrival said. "We are going to have to have a system for this. I am me; just me." Fright and fear had turned to pedantic ire, and Ms. De Beer wanted ever so much at that moment to be the only her.

"Me too," the other Ms. De Beer replied.

The lamplight shuddered with the air escaping through the door, and Ms. De Beer had an idea that would hopefully save some confusion.

"Alright, well in that case I think we'll have to call you something else."

"You mean call you something else?"

"No, you. You will be called 'Me-Two'," said Ms. De Beer, and she looked for signs of confusion on the face of her host.

"I don't suppose we can call each other 'Ms. De Beer' all the time, and you seem so unsettled, I wouldn't like to be like you," the copy replied.

Ms. De Beer was slightly offended, but she decided to err on the side of politeness and ignore her host's rude observation and smooth it over with grudging assent. This was all bringing to mind those terribly bleak fables that the parents, which she must have had at some point, had read to her. Parents, she had learned from television and films, were in the habit of trying to scare morals into their children with just such stories, and, well, she just wasn't having it. If life was to be a fable, to be built on fiction, then she decided she would have to write it herself. She would be a revisionist, and she would have her revenge on history once this was all sorted out.

There was a crack of thunder outside then, or perhaps it was noise of a feathery thing that flew in the sky bumping into a wooden thing that rudely went silent during conversation. Whatever it was, Me-Two jumped and shook, and looked around in vain for something to hide behind. Ms. De Beer was not at all worried by the things that went bump in the night, and she looked at her other self with surprise and not a little disappointment. Why would I be scared? Why would I let the unknown get in my head and taunt me into fear?

Why indeed.

She tried to distract Me-Two by asking a polite question.

"How did you get here?"

Me-Two, still agitated but warming with the idea that someone wanted to know something about her, stuttered into speech.

"I arrived on a very nice boat, it was kind enough to bring me to the shore on the other side of the island, and the house."

"What do you mean by nice exactly?" Ms. De Beer the First was not a little taken aback that Me-Two's boat had been nice, but before she could get really offended she would need to know what she meant by 'nice'. This odd, easily-scared reflection could find sinking ships nice, if they got where they were going before they sank, and if that were the case then Ms. De Beer would be mentally preening and safe in the knowledge that her idea of nice was, in fact, the nicer nice.

"Well. It had the loveliest soft velvet seats, and there was a bar with all sorts of coloured liqueurs, although I don't drink, but the colours were pretty. There were oars too, and they were moving by themselves, and I just knew they'd steer me right. It was all very plush and, well, safe! I do like to feel safe, and there was no moving off until I said to! Such a gentleman, that boat."

Ms. De Beer was not happy. This was definitely falling into the basket marked 'what's wrong with me, then?', but she was adamant she would rise above it.

"What was your boat like?' asked Me-Two.

"That's really beside the point. My boat didn't have to be asked to move, it had the good sense to know what to do, and it only talked very little, so really I think you got the bum deal here." Ms. De Beer was not happy at all.

The two of her were still standing at the door, one on the soft rug of the entryway, one still stifling the step. The step had stayed quiet, not finding an appropriate break in the discussion to point out that the boots on its head were going to leave permanent grooves and grids if they weren't promptly removed. The nature outside the door was getting impatient too. When a door stayed open that long, the outside tried to get inside for lack of another way to go. Up was good, and down, but in was the best of all the directions, and it was all it could do not to snake around the ankles of both of the woman and creep across the floors and up the walls.

Shut the door, shut it now or we will come in and there will be no in.

Ms. De Beer, cold all of a sudden and very aware of her lake-soaked trousers and soggy boots, gave Me-Two that look that one gives people when something has been missed, something important and really rather unavoidable. Me-Two tilted her head to the side, puppyish and fuddled, and had an idea that she may not have had otherwise.

"Oh! But you're wet, and it's cold. Come in and we'll get settled."

About time.

Boats almost forgotten, the plural woman went in and closed the door. Vines subsided, crept back to the places they could find root, and the night closed in against its seams.

The room turned out not to be an entryway at all, and among the dust and old chairs Ms. De Beer and Me-Two were rather closer to each other than Ms. De Beer would have liked.

Ms. De Beer approvingly noted the faded print of cabbage roses on the wallpaper as she appraised the space. The ceiling was very high, and there were cobwebs hanging down almost to the top of the fireplace. Both the woman had tried to take the seat closest to the fireplace, what with it being the warmest spot, but after the 'polite dance of who is going which way', Ms. De Beer had won the day and was sitting in an uncomfortable armchair, a large spring from the depths of the upholstery jutting into her arse most unapologetically.

"I do need to dry off you know, I got quite damp getting out of my boat."

"It's only your trouser legs and your shoes, really not that bad at all, and there are plenty of dry clothes you could change into. They are in the next room back though, could take you a while to get in there."

Ms. De Beer was about to be pleased that there were other rooms, presumably ones where she could retreat from Me-Two and have a proper think about the day's events, when she stopped and asked, "What do you mean, it could take me a while?"

"The rooms here are very particular," said Me-Two. "You can only go through the next door when you've done the thing you were meant to do, and not before."

Ms. De Beer exhaled loudly and tugged her damp boots off her tired feet. As she bent to do so, pairs of pebbles tumbled from her pockets onto the threadbare rug and got themselves all out of order. They seemed to be duller, seemed to be taking too much of the room in, so she left them where they lay.

"And just what do you mean by 'the next room back'? I am moving forwards, and I will continue to do so."

"Oh, no, oh gosh I should have said. You've come in the back door!" Me-Two's voice was beginning to take on that tone that people use to talk to babies and cats.

Ms. De Beer was sure that both the cats and the babies were annoyed by it, and she was certainly starting to feel that way herself. Me-Two continued though, unaware that somewhere, in the depths of the house, her high-pitched sing-songing was probably breaking some poor little mouse family's best glassware.

"No, this is definitely the back room. I came in the front on the other side of the island, and I've been working my way through the rooms ever since! It really is a lovely old house, but I will be rather glad to get home again. I must tell my doctor that I've started seeing purple!"

"Oh? Been to the doctor lately have you?" Ms. De Beer was trying very hard not to seem overly interested in the fact that the other her had also been to a doctor, and also appeared to be having trouble with colour, and she mostly succeeded. Partly she was angry that this badly wrought double was using her problem as its own, and partly she was happy that someone else couldn't see this 'red' thing.

"Yes, well I was really having trouble with SAD."

"Oh, dear, yes depression is a terrible thing..."

"Oh, well yes, but when I say 'sad' I mean SAD –

Seasonal Affective Disorder. All these grey days we've had, and so many in a row, well they just eat away at me after a while. It's got to the point that I'm almost ready to stop looking up at all."

Grey days? What was this flibbertigibbet talking about? Days in these parts mostly dawned high and clear, and stayed that way, painfully bright blue, until the sun waltzed in and sorted it out.

"Anyway, the doctor said that it wasn't SAD, more that I was having trouble with something called 'blues', or 'blue' maybe. Either way, it seems I can't see it so he's sent me off on a diet of blueberries, whatever they are, and bubble-gum flavoured jellybeans, which is playing havoc on my dental care routine to say the least!"

Me-Two slumped back in her seat (the one not all that close to the fire), a bit tuckered out and breathless from her little explosion of information. Talking about herself always seemed such a guilty pleasure, such a chocolate biscuit in a world of crackers, that she almost always tripped over herself and let it all come out too fast. Now she was tired, and ready to sleep, and beginning to be grateful that this other her was coming in as she was getting ready to leave.

Ms. De Beer was intrigued, oh yes, because she had the ability to see blue – ha, she had it! This daft wretch was without blue and she'd known they weren't one and the same, she'd known it right from when the door opened and her silly, twee expression had looked back at her from familiar brows and eyes and freckles.

"Oh, that's, uh, interesting you should say that, as I've been to the doctor myself lately for an issue of a colourful nature, or colourless perhaps. It seems I am unable to see something called 'red'. I had been enquiring as to the possibility of having my eyes removed, but of course that all fell to bits. I'm on cherries and rare steak myself, much healthier." Ms. De Beer was suitably puffed up and ready to crow that her doctor had seen fit to be so dedicated to her health, forgetting of course that that was what they were supposed to do, and that really, Me-Two's doctor hadn't had a lot of choice in the prescription department when it came to blue foods. There were only so many blueberries a person could eat before things got uncomfortable indeed.

"Yes, well, it's getting late..." Me-Two's voice trailed off and she glanced longingly at the camp bed in the corner. If she was going to figure out how to get out of here in the morning, she'd need to get some rest.

Both of the woman found a bed, one on the camp bed, the other on an overstuffed old mattress on the floor, and they each set about their nighttime routines. Ms. De Beer, finding that the little sink in the corner was actually working, decided to brush her teeth. Me-Two, being aware that the plumbing in the old house was notoriously temperamental, decided against doing the same, choosing instead to fold herself into the blankets and hope that she would dream about the way out while she slept.

"Hey, here's a thing," said Ms. De Beer, suddenly confused, and not just by the strange purple water coming out of the taps. "Why didn't you leave when you let me in? The door was open, you could have slung your hook right then and headed off home!"

It was quiet for a moment, and then there could be heard a rather exasperated sigh, as if Me-Two were sick of her cats-and-babies routine and would just like this person to shut up now.

Shut up now.

"Can't, doesn't work that way. Had I walked out, there would only have ended up being another door somewhere, and probably a trickier one at that. No, best to follow the rules on this path."

Chapter Three

Dawn must have broken at some point, but the shabby little window, shaded as it was by the gnarled old forest outside, hadn't had the opportunity to throw light at either of the sleeping people in the first-last room. The little window never got to do that, never got to throw the light, it only ever got to catch it from inside the house, and by then it was already caught really, so there was no fun in that. The house, finished with its ins-and-outs for the night, straightened and flexed and was all of a sudden a bit higher, holding its breath for the day's puzzles and punctures, about to stifle a 12-hour yawn.

Me-Two was an early riser, and had already eaten breakfast and begun working on the door and its required task before Ms. De Beer had even begun to snuffle and wriggle and crack open an eyelid. Snuffle and wriggle and crack she did, eventually and all of a sudden, and felt a bit as though she'd slept through her alarm, or missed a wedding, or worse, a funeral. Once she had rearranged herself into something that looked as grim and severe as she hoped she did, she stood and wandered over to where Me-Two was gazing at the wallpaper. It wasn't roses after all, she noticed, the pattern was lavender, which was not a bit as nice as roses.

Ms. De Beer noticed Me-Two's empty breakfast plate dangling precariously from the very small window-sill (another sore point for the window), and her stomach grumbled quietly.

"Is there any more food?" she asked politely, although it would have been much better had she remembered to say good morning to her fellow house guest.

"Oh, good morning!" Me-Two turned abruptly, limbs all noodly and wobbling like a wet dog, and she knocked her plate clean off the sill. "Oops, I'm always bloody well doing that."

Ms. De Beer was slightly shocked at the casual swearing, especially as they'd only just met, but she'd been known to utter a few choice curse words herself, and Me-Two was herself, so she forgave them both and moved on to more breakfast-y things.

"Ah well, no matter, accidents happen," she said brightly, not wanting to offend Me-Two into withholding important food information.

"Yes, they do seem to happen. Quite often actually. And always something sharp too..."

Ms. De Beer followed Me-Two's gaze to the other woman's arm, and although she couldn't clearly see the pale pink criss-crossing of the scars along that arm, she could certainly make out that there were too many edges on something that shouldn't have an edge at all. This version obviously let life get in more often than was healthy, the poor dear.

"Gosh, I bet you can't wait to get away from here," said Ms. De Beer, enjoying as she was the thought of doing it herself.

"Away? Oh goodness no, I'm not going away, I'm going 'to'! I never go away, I hate to say goodbye, so I go to, because then I never have to go away, and, oh it makes sense in my head anyway..."

Ms. De Beer doubted very much whether anything in Me-Two's head made sense, and if it did it was likely the things she'd borrowed from other heads, or from things like clocks and radios that just do the thing and don't have to make sense – they are the sense.

The woman to the power of two both sat and contemplated anything but each other. Ms. De Beer was very keen to get through the first door, but not until Me-Two had left – she didn't want anyone seeing her skittering around the room in thought, and she almost always skittered when she was contained during the thinking of things.

Ms. De Beer contained her skittering with a half-hearted search for food. Finding only another bare plate, she sat down and contemplated it. It was empty, save for a blurry thing, a stalk jutting from the smudge with a tiny, browning leaf attached. Her doctor had told her to look out for just such a smudge, and so she was fairly sure that she was having an apple for breakfast. She bit down, and there was definitely something to it, a resistance there that wouldn't have been so were it not real, but under that it was floury, the inside as old and faded as the outside.

"Oh, you got an apple. That's nice," said Me-Two, almost done with her murky coffee. She was back to staring intently at the door again, carefully considering its lines and gaps, and the way it let a bit of light through if she looked at it on the right angle.

"Oh, is it an apple?" Ms. De Beer replied, quietly stoking her brain awake with her rightness and her coffee. "It's a bit old I think, tastes like juicy dust with skin, but it'll do for now."

Me-Two had moved on though, the apple being nothing extraordinary for her, and she continued to watch the thin sliver of light play across the floor. It was time to get this door open.

An old rag lay near the exit, just below the sill of the small window (who had embarrassingly dropped it some days before on account of a gust of wind and lack of surface area). Me-Two picked it up, shook off the dust and a piece of grit or two, then set about giving the door's metal fixtures a rather good spit-shine. Each expulsion of dribble from her mouth seemed to coincide with Ms. De Beer's next mouthful, both strangely wet, but one going in and the other coming out.

The fixtures gleamed under the crack of light's approving gaze, so Me-Two moved on to dusting the wooden panels, not with the spit mind you, that would be quite rude. One should never attempt to fix another's countenance with the spittle of one's own; at least that was what she thought. Did she?

She hadn't actually thought that until now, and Ms. De Beer, watching from behind what was now the core of a smudge, recognised the peculiar shift crossing Me-Two's face. She'd seen it often enough, in shop windows when she was walking and looked up, catching herself deep in thought. Once, she had sat in front of the old mirror that had come with her house and really watched herself think. She had noted the brows that never seemed to relax, the eyes that didn't see unless directly told to, and the mouth twisted slightly open so as to breathe – goodness knows her nose had never seemed up to the job.

The wood of the front-back door began to warm under Me-Two's tender dusting and polishing. The crack of light grew wider, and a faint click could most definitely be heard from the snib of the door handle. It seemed she had done the thing, and that the door would open and she would be able to go to wherever it was she was from. Certainly not away from here, just to home. Ms. De Beer had a sudden urge to stride over and pull the door to its widest opening, to step out into the morning light before Me-Two could even put down the rag and gather her things to depart. They looked so similar – surely the door, which was without eyes, or whiskers for felt-things or a nose for smelt-things, would have some trouble telling the difference between them? Ms. De Beer did not stride over to the door, and she did not try to get out before

Me-Two. The poor thing was obviously a bit potty for having been here for – how long had she been in this place?

"Weeks, I think," said Me-Two, answering the silent question. "There really are a few rooms to get through, depending on how the house feels of course, and there didn't seem to be a rush."

Ms. De Beer, shocked at both the question's soundless journey and the answer, bit the side of her tongue and resolved that she would not be here for more than a few days at best, a week if she must stay any longer than that. She must get away.

As the them spoke and thought, the door creaked open just far enough to allow Me-Two to wedge her foot, and her leg up to mid-calf, through and out onto the step. Foot out and foot in, she scrabbled and reached across the floor to grab her modest bag of things that hadn't turned out to be very useful at all. She had brought a pen, which promised to be useful but ended up being quite a waste of limited bag-space, as well as some hand lotion, a bunch of keys she'd found in her back garden (also useless), and a little bottle of rosewater. None of her things had been of any help, excepting the fact that they were there and they were hers, and she supposed that made them at least a tiny bit helpful in the end. She still had somewhere to go, though, and they could very well end up being useful there.

With her foot firmly planted on the step, Me-Two continued to polish the door panels, and after a time she thought that perhaps, if she swapped the rag to her other hand, she might be able to slip her arm around the door's edge and administer some attention to the other side of it. The door, having predicted her thought before she'd even thought it, creaked open ever so slightly more, and the wood of its frontliness began to colour and deepen in its glow as it was de-cobwebbed and divested of the spots and blemishes that the elements had left behind. The door didn't think the elements would mind – they'd be back as soon as the cleaning was done, sending spiders and gentle breezes that carried the tiniest of specks. They might even send a vine or two to draw itself in 3D up the step and onto the clean slate. There was plenty of time.

As each part of the door's front became cleaner, it would open just a tiny crack to admit more of Me-Two's body to the outside. Very soon, only her head was left in the room, and she awkwardly flung her arms, stretching to reach the last freckles of forest-y filth from about the door's person. She considered, albeit briefly, using her foot to flick the final bits clean, but she knew that she would fall, and that the door would close on her if she did that, so she continued to strain her joints into letting her limbs move further than was really a good idea. Her elbows cracked, her shoulders made a noise that only dogs could hear, and her knees were about to take their caps off and throw them to the dust.

This was a time to push though, and she did. While she did so, while her spongy seams were all but tearing, Ms. De Beer was watching on, quite bored if she were to be honest. She was fighting off the urge to smoke, still letting the rules of second-hand smoke make first-hand demands, but they were getting weaker and so was she. Just as Me-Two's head was the only part of her still in the room, Ms. De Beer decided that perhaps the rules could be broken, that she could light up a coffin nail and blow the smoke up the chimney, and that would be quite considerate enough.

"Look at that, you're out! You won't mind, now that you're free to go, if I light a cigarette? Of course not, and do travel well, you've earned it!"

As she spat out the niceties she turned, pressing a cigarette between her pouting lips, raising her lighter quicker than a hummingbird's wings could flap. The smoke curled to the ceiling, wafted towards the door, and its tendrils began to stroke the wooden panels.

Me-Two had not the time or the breath to explain that she wasn't quite out yet, and that she'd really rather prefer it if Ms. De Beer could refrain from smoking until she had reunited her head with the rest of her bits. She had neither the time or the breath because the door, pushed by the little hazy hands of smoke, had begun to press across her neck, squeezing all her good work out of her mouth before she could trap it back in. Outside the door, her limbs began to wobble and twitch at the stoppage of air, and inside the door her face began to go a shade of blue that she could not have seen had she tried.

Ms. De Beer was curled inwards to the smoke's outward arc, scrunched just so and blowing her dying breaths toward the chimney after each greedy inward heave. The air was silent with it, and she had assumed that Me-Two was gone, skipping onwards on her merry way like a bobble-headed carbon copy, the ink shifted and fattened and not quite the same. Yes, she had gone, so Ms. De Beer could indulge, and she always thought the best when she could sit and indulge. The earth didn't seem to pulse so much when one had a cigarette to suck on, and she imagined she looked like a frustrated writer, all sophisticated and waiting for the bolt to smack her in the head and show her the way. She was missing it all, she was missing the blue of Me-Two's quickly fading spark as it leeched over the panels of the door and swept up the last of the dust. Life has a way of creeping over everything when your heart can't hold it anymore, and Me-Two's was following the smoke's veiny path right out the door and into the trees. Her life floated in formation, tiny bubbles of stuff catching under the leaves and snagging on twigs, and it looked for all the world as if it was snowing upwards, if such a thing were possible.

Chapter Four

Me-Two had gone, in a way. She had sputtered out her final breath as her limbs danced and danced and tried to coax it back. The breath was already mingling with the breaths of a countless band of souls no-longer-upright, not at all keen to nip back and try to prop up a whole person on its own. The breaths chattered in the canopy as they rose, and the limbs fell ground-ward, grazing the step with their halt. Knowing they wouldn't move without some help, the step settled in for a long wait, hoping the decay wouldn't mess up his slate-grey top too much. It was always such an effort to find enough new feet to shudder the bones of the old ones off and cross the threshold without making unpleasant noises.

The air changed, and the smoke didn't curl so much as flee. Ms. De Beer was almost at the end of her second cigarette, and was seriously contemplating a third when she finally turned back to the door. Me-Two's wide, dead eyes and blue-ish head accused her from the jamb of the doorway, and she jumped up open-mouthed, her sudden intake of breath catching the cigarette smoke half up and half down her windpipe. It wasn't sure which way to go, so it set her to coughing and spluttering with force enough to decide either way, eventually. Ms. De Beer stood shaking, clutching at her chest, cradling her own lack of breath in her trembling hands, and felt the first seedlings of guilt push their dirty heads through her shock. For the life of her she didn't know how this could have happened to the life of HER. She had been poised to triumph, to step out into the world with new resolve and the battle won, but now she was sucked back into the room, the flood-waters bringing the mud of regret in with their sediment. It would all need cleaning off, especially the sadness.

She supposed she wasn't sorry that the other one was dead, but she might have been a touch sorry that she hadn't noticed her in the dying of it. Leaving the world with nothing but the back of your reflection to gaze at seemed a bit harsh, and she was sorry for that. The door wouldn't have moved had she seen, she was sure of that, and she was also sure that there was nothing she could have done to save Me-Two.

Quite sure. Stop asking questions.

Ms. De Beer stubbed out her cigarette on the hearth, and the floor shuddered slightly, as if the tiny burn was enough to make it flinch. The door swung open, wide and wild, enticing the smoke to rush out in one big puff of its hinges. The little window rattled in reply, not quite sure how it was going to get out the smell, but pleased that at the very least it had been involved with the rest of the house for a moment. The walls always let it join in, sometimes when it didn't want to. The times that it wanted to join in were the best, but even the moments that it buckled without consent, well at least it was doing something, was part of something.

It wasn't even lunchtime and the silly woman was dead.

Ms. De Beer couldn't stop looking at the head in the door. Its peepers were open, stubbornly refusing to blink themselves into sleep, and the green eyes were slowly becoming more purple each time Ms. De Beer looked again. Every second, every flutter of eyelids, brought further purpling, the eyes as bruised as the lake. She couldn't look again, but did, and before long, or even after quite long, it was well after lunchtime. There was something about the purple eyes that made her stay just where she was. She had not dared to light another cigarette, although the door wouldn't have minded now. Well, that particular door wouldn't have minded. There would be much energy expended convincing the next door, the one that led away, to open itself.

Chapter Five

Ms. De Beer had spent the whole afternoon trying not to look at, and also looking at, the dead head in the doorframe. She had thought that perhaps if she got up and moved to her mattress on the floor, or tried to do the dishes, that she could stop looking at it long enough to break the wispy chain that had been connecting her eyes to the blue face all day so far. Doing the dishes had been a fruitless endeavour – she had turned on the tap and instead of purple water, out spouted a blur of other blurs, a rope of smudged something that ran into the sink and piled up like a coiled snake, unable to bite but unsettling nonetheless.

The day was cooling, preparing the edges of the world for the arrival of night, and Ms. De Beer did not like the idea of sleeping in a room with a slightly open door and a floating dead head. Death was one thing, but she wouldn't be able to sleep in the knowledge that the bloody, blinking door was open.

She dragged a chair over to the door and pushed its heavy frame against the panels, which was ruder than she'd ever been in her whole entire life. She was further squashing poor Me-Two's neck between the door and the frame. The indignity of it was not lost on her, but she decided that the dead woman would not want anyone to suffer in her wake, as dead people are often heard to remark after death, usually from the mouths of people who want to do things that they may not have liked in life. Her guilt fought with her delusion instead of driving her actions, and she had a balance of sorts. Too many tightropes and not enough umbrellas, though, when it came down to it, and she could only balance on one of them at a time.

The door, unusually accommodating with this sudden extra weight and promise of closure, took its lead from Ms. De Beer, shifting itself further forward with immense but gradual force. It was glad that the live one wasn't trying to make her escape, as per the rules, and it had only held off from a proper, jarring slam because it felt that perhaps it wouldn't have been polite to cause further damage to the dead one. The live one might have been sad, might have cried or something, or perhaps broken down the door, and in all the door's time here there had only been one person to do that, and he'd ended up impaled on a large, sharp pointy bit that he'd created in his destruction. It had been a messy business all round.

There was a slow crunch, with a slight squelch, and then a very loud fast one. The door was closed, and Me-Two's head was rolling across the floor towards the retreating feet of Ms. De Beer. She had been about to apply herself to the opening of the next door, and the little bump to the back of her boots went unnoticed for a moment. When she turned she didn't so much as gasp but gurgle, a wet bubble of shock rose from her stomach halfway up her windpipe, and she felt she was about to surrender up the apple she'd had for breakfast. Almost. Not quite.

Ms. De Beer really wasn't sure what the standard response was to finding a severed head at your feet. She sort of nudged it with her boot, just a bit, and certainly not enough to be disrespectful at all. Not at all. The rag, still at the door, got a bit bigger in its usefulness, and in doing so she saw it. She picked it up and draped it over the should-be-grim-but-quite-pretty face staring up at her, then sat down in the chair next to the now cold fireplace and took stock of things. Then she shifted to the chair that was not quite as close to the fireplace, because it seemed as if she were rubbing it in, and that maybe she should let the head have that spot. Better yet, the grate was cold, the embers of the fire long gone, she could put the head in the fireplace, a sort of cremation, or one promised, or something.

She scooped her hand under the head, avoiding the oozing blur that seemed to be running from its neck, and quickly carried it to the fireplace, rag still intact. The floor had become quite indistinct with whatever it was that was coming from the head, and there was a definite hazy patch on the floor by the door, long thin tendrils of the smudginess tracing the path that the head had rolled to get to her feet.

Ms. De Beer sat again in the chair closest to the fireplace. Me-Two, or part of her at least, was now even closer to it than she, so it seemed as though it'd be ok for her to sit there now. She sat, barely looking but eyes turned to the head, for some hours. It was enough hours for the sky to darken outside the little sad window, the sun going down on another day without so much as throwing a ray at its window-pain.

By the time night had painted itself across the trees and vines, had tethered the outside with the weight of slumber, Ms. De Beer had fallen into a fitful sleep of her own in the tatty chair, twisted leg and hand propping cheek like a very fleshy statue, and an unfinished one at that. The house gently rocked, pulsing in rhythm with Ms. De Beer's weak, weary heart, and the lavender on the walls took the same journey as the old fashioned cabbage roses had the previous night – up, and spongily over, seeping through the doorframe and into the next room.

Chapter Six

Ms. De Beer woke before the sun, so she didn't notice the freesias on the wallpaper until the light had started to filter through the crevices of the room. Much better than lavender anyway, so there was at least something pleasant to the start of the day. This morning's breakfast had been blueberries, which was a bit unsettling under the circumstances, but she was hungry so she ate them without too much thought as to who they were intended for.

Breakfast wasn't the thing anyway, the important thing. Breakfast was the thing before the important thing, and now was the time for that thing to happen. She would apply herself most diligently to the opening of the next door, and her days in the house would be numbered much fewer than the tragic Me-Two's had totalled before her entirely accidental, really-couldn't-have-helped-at-all demise.

She hadn't smoked yet that morning, though the craving leapt in her brain and danced through her veins. Could she risk it? Well that was the thing, she didn't know, so a good part of the morning was spent in the pursuit of being about to do something, then not doing it, her eyes resting on the cigarette pouch instead of the door. All the almost-doing and not-doing wore at the door, and it thought perhaps hope might banish tobacco from Ms. De Beer's mind, although it didn't know her name, it just thought of her as the grumpy one. The door was bored, and impatient, and hadn't had to wait nearly this long for the sillier one to work it out. It was different for this one though – it was always different. You never knew just how the tilt of a hinge or the warp of the humid air would change the way the door opened, but it did open now, just a crack and of its own accord, and with a tiny creak to announce that it was helping.

Ms. De Beer heard the creak, she had heard it, but she wasn't about to be pulled into the hopeful orbit that had killed Me-Two. Absolutely not. She stole a quick peek at the frame of door-the-second, and knew that its being open wasn't so much an invitation as encouragement. She would take the encouragement, oh yes she would, but she wouldn't let it hoodwink her into pushing any part of herself through before she was ready, before it was wide enough to admit the all of her.

The day was mostly spent diligently doing things that didn't work. Ms. De Beer, tiny screwdriver from her glasses case in hand, had tried to prod every tiny hole in the room, hoping for a secret latch or a spring mechanism. She'd spent rather a long time doing that, and the door was finding it rather amusing. She was, instead of searching for the needle, using it to perforate the haystack, and it wasn't working. It didn't work the first time, and the door, and even the sad little window, thought that perhaps she would have worked that out sooner than she did. When she finally did concede and stop the prodding, it was night again. A whole day wasted putting things into places that didn't want them, and that weren't quite the right fit anyway.

"This is ridiculous, I'm never going to get through!" Ms. De Beer screamed at the head in the fireplace.

While not replying in the traditional sense, under the rag the crooked dead mouth of Me-Two withered a bit, puckered at the raising of voice, and if Ms. De Beer had looked it might have been akin to a smile. The rag twitched, and Ms. De Beer lost her temper properly then, got all flustered and picked up the head. She stuffed it into her bag and strode to the door, grabbing her now-empty plate (stained as it was with blueberry juice) and a blanket from her lumpy mattress of the past two nights. She stood at the door defiant.

"I am coming through, and I am bringing the head because it wouldn't do to leave it here in this silly place."

The door opened. It actually flipping opened.

Ms. De Beer was surprised at the force of her surprise, and its language, but that was not to be worried about until she was through the door.

"I'm coming through now, please don't close on me or do anything nasty, I'm just walking through, nothing more." Ms. De Beer's voice wasn't quivering as much as it should have, and the door was seriously considering slamming on her as she passed through.

She ran though, she ran with a severed head and a bag full of tat, ran like a child runs when the day has promised things and means to make good on it. She was faster than she looked.

She ran so swiftly that she brought the dust of the old room into the new room, and as the door slammed behind her and her bag and the head and the blanket, the dust complained and tried to make friends with the new colony of motes that danced in the light of the space.

The new room was vast. It spread out so high and wide that Ms. De Beer felt very small and altogether too out in the open. She moved to the nearest corner and sat on the bare floorboards, scanning the whole thing for unknown threats. There was nothing in the room for the most part, but that didn't calm her at all, it was only fuel for a futile fire that would burn more in the synapses than it ever would in the air. And there was a lot of air. Almost too much for one pair of lungs to process.

As Ms. De Beer calmed herself in her little corner, which actually made the vast vaster if she was to think about it, she noticed the walls were off. Off in the sense that they shifted like oil on water, not so greasy or covered in filthy rainbows, but they were ill-defined and swimming in their own solidity. The next door, way down the other end of the cleverly-wrought and horribly-thought space, was doing the same, only obviously an actual door because there was a handle and a step. The step was going up.

Not only was the step going up, the walls moving and whirling, but there were vines and leaves, and was that a tree? The new door looked like the outside of the first door, and it was quite clever how much detail the house had elected to keep in. That was commitment right there. Ms. De Beer knew, without really thinking about it, that this was the outside come in, and she recognised the step and door handle and the panels she had knocked on, though they were misty now.

The step was very pleased indeed! It was inside – in! It was a very rare thing to be on the inside, and it was going to enjoy this. They never got through the door very quickly, always made a mistake before the final turning of the knob, and it was looking forward to at least a week without the elements chattering in the night and staining its slate top with dusty life-prints. Life-prints were sticky buggers.

So vast was the room, and so accurate the reproduction of the outside-in, that Ms. De Beer wasn't sure if what she was seeing was what she was seeing. It certainly appeared to be an exact replica of the outside of the inside, but she thought perhaps she should check. Her eyes played tricks on her as she walked the boards to the other end of the enormous room, and the shifting and mottling of the walls certainly wasn't helping her to focus.

The thing that worried her, well it was the thing on the step. There was a thing that seemed to have arms, and legs, and shoulders and all the other requisite bits, and it was lying on the step just as she imagined it should have been on the outside. The thing was though, was that it didn't have a head. Ms. De Beer neared the thing on the step and tried to be horrified that she recognised the trousers and shirt lying step-wards, but she wasn't really. She wasn't even a bit surprised. Bodies seemed to follow heads, in her experience, and she had brought the head with her, brought it through stuffed in her bag like an overripe melon, indistinct seeds weeping through the lining.

This was quite the problem. She would need to move the body before she could do anything about the door, before she could take the 'up' the step was silently offering and unlock the next room. She must move it, yes, but she didn't really want to touch the thing. Even without a head it seemed to be looking at her, each fingernail a little ocular substitute, gleaming wetly just as an eyeball would.

Chapter Seven

Just for a minute, Ms. De Beer thought that she'd get right on it – she would sort this blasted door out right now, and then perhaps the next would be a bit easier – less death with any luck. There was still the matter of the headless Me-Two to deal with though, and that unsavoury task, the moving of the body, arrested her progress no small amount. It was one thing to pick up something small and dead, say a severed head for instance, but pulling a body from its final stop on the road, to remove it from the place it had chosen to rest, well that was a philosophical dilemma.

Ms. De Beer regularly became philosophical when faced with a hard choice. Why, surely it was better to ponder matters to their core, to pierce their marrow and count their bones, before one got to the stage of actually doing something? Was doing something even the point, if the thoughts were noble and the mind all a-canter? Ms. De Beer often avoided doing something using just this method, but it didn't seem to be working in the usual fashion today. She would have to do the thing.

Yes, now was the time to do the thing, so she stepped closer to the corpse in order to ascertain just how much nature she'd have to relocate before she could slide it away from the door. There wasn't much – a couple of cheeky-green vines with tear-drop leaves rested across one of Me-Two's former legs, and a big stick lay across one of the hands, looking for all the world as if it were spoiling for a fight. It was altogether spooky, the effect of them together, but they would be easily moved and then she'd only have the residual spookiness of a dead body, sans head, to deal with.

It was actual, real, syrupy night now. Although it was hard to tell without a bare window to frame the real, syrupy outside. It could have been the hour before the sun rises again, or it could have been the moment before crickets start up their noise, or it could be day again and she just didn't know it yet. Whatever time it was, it was the time for sleeping, and her weary limbs sent her all kinds of little impulses, up her nerve-ways to her brain, knocking on their own wee door and begging to be let in for a rest and some of the sweet darkness that hid up there in the corners of the twisted grey. She gave in soon enough, and went back to her corner where the walls met and danced.

She had her blanket, but there was no camp bed or mattress in here. The floorboards weren't too bad, she supposed, and she tried to arrange herself into something resembling comfort, the blanket rolled in places, flattened in others, trying to act as pillow and covering and buffer all at the same time. This turned out to be another thing to add to the list of things that didn't work.

Ms. De Beer watched the other end of the room, wary and weary and not sure what nature would do with the body on the step if she were to sleep. It looked cold too, slapped onto the cold slate step like that. She knew that being cold was part of being dead – she had once watched a documentary on such things – still she couldn't help but feel a sympathetic something for the corpse that she hadn't felt at all when it wasn't a corpse. This would not do at all.

Ms. De Beer rose from the floorboards, dragging the blanket up with her by a frayed corner, and strode back down the length of the room to the step. She had decided to move the body, and so she bent to it, gently slipping her hands under the arms and pulling ever so carefully. It would also not do for the arms to come off as well.

Sleeping follicles woke, and each tiny hair, each tufty, downy thing on Me-Two's shrinking skin was stirred to action. As Ms. De Beer pulled, they set to pushing, the softest of skitters and patters across the floor. Moving the body was easier than Ms. De Beer had thought it would be, what with the invisible assistance of the helpful hairs, and the little window watched her slide past. It felt a kind of kinship with her then, in that they'd both moved something, and that they'd both been surprised at their own strength. It would have liked to throw her some light to see better by.

Ms. De Beer pulled the body some metres away from the step and the door, and laid it on its back. She crossed its arms over the deflated chest, and was almost happy with having done the thing. But the thing wasn't really done, she now saw, the thing had changed entirely. The thing now would be to rescue the head from her bag and restore it to its place, atop the crusting neck of the body.

Ms. De Beer dug in her shallow bag and found the head, although her screwdriver had somehow become wedged in an eye. Surely this was Me-Two making jokes at her from the grave? Well, it would have been the grave had it been buried, but Ms. De Beer was sure that she knew what she meant. Either way, dead or not, it was rude. She removed the screwdriver from the unblinking blinker and the head from the bag, and took it to the body.

It looked much less 'off' now, with the head sitting neatly flush with the neck. Although Ms. De Beer couldn't get the head to stay eyes-up – it would loll one way or the other, using an ear either side as a makeshift stand. She positioned the head so it was looking away, no, 'to' the door, and not at Ms. De Beer herself. Next was the blanket. Ms. De Beer tucked Me-Two in, and once she had arranged the fabric just so, well you'd never have been able to tell that she was dead at all! Sick maybe, what with the blueness and the spongy texture of the skin, but yes, she looked as though she had a head that was attached to her body, and that she was at the very least comfortably sleeping.

Though she knew it wasn't true, appearances being what they were made Ms. De Beer feel much more comfortable herself. Even without a blanket, only the blurry walls to lean against with their barely perceptible pulse, she was feeling just about ready to sleep. It must be night still, or near enough to it to warrant putting one's head up against the wall for a quiet moment and hopefully some more again. Her eyelashes came together, and their gossiping replaced the chatter in Ms. De Beer's head, and she was almost, very nearly asleep when it happened again.

There was a very small creak in the very big room, but it was enough to admit some new air and let out some nature. Ms. De Beer stirred slightly, but she wasn't quite awake, or quite asleep. She was quite unsure as to whether she'd heard the creak, and she wasn't in the mood to have her hopes dashed, so she stayed put. Minutes passed quickly, their ticking heads turning only very briefly to see the woman in the corner twitch and dribble, and to wonder why she hadn't been clever enough to catch a few of them as they went. Minutes were about the best things to catch, unless you were a window. Snatch a moment and you'd have it forever.

Eventually the walls grew tired of the stand-off, and began to pulse all the more in an attempt to get Ms. De Beer on her feet and across the room. The floorboards agreed, and they rolled gently under the arse of Ms. De Beer, which had been a bit bony for them if the truth be told. Needs must when there's a pointy bottom digging into your planks.

Ms. De Beer rose sluggishly, still foggy enough with impending sleep that her legs were able to navigate the swell of the floor. She floated to the door on ripples of wood, and before long was peering at the small gap the creak had been talking about. She reached for the knob, and she pulled just a little, but it wasn't going to move that easily, goodness no. There was something she was forgetting, that much was clear.

She'd forgotten her bag anyway, and she'd need that, though her phone was out of battery and the rest of her things hadn't helped at all. Just like Me-Two's bag-of-nothing-good-at-all. Where was that bag? She'd had it when she'd popped her body out the door hadn't she? And it was there, under a pile of leaves and bug-bedding was the satchel with things in it that could be left, but shouldn't be left. Ms. De Beer wondered just how much she was expected to collect and take with her before she could walk out into the outside air.

She picked up Me-Two's bag, and as it was impractical and small she decided she could put in her own bag. She tried the doorknob again, but it was stubbornly refusing to move, knowing as it did that she had forgotten another thing – the actual thing.

"Ah," said Ms. De Beer with a hint of trouble about her tone. "I have to take her."

It wasn't a question.

She had worked out the thing, and so she set about

working out how she was going to do the thing. How did one move a headless corpse, and its head, from one room to another, as well as two bags and a blanket?

A blanket! There was a bloody, sodding, blinking blanket, and it would be saving the day instead of only coming out at night. Ms. De Beer scurried back to the body-and-head of Me-Two and pulled the blanket from its tucked-in places.

Blanket spread floorwards and ready to receive, she again slipped her hands under the arms of her dead-friend and began to lift. The hairs weren't much use this time, they pushed off a bit, that was true, and a bit of extra momentum never hurt on starting off a big job, but once their length had been expended they hung limp and useless in the breeze that snuck through the crack in the door.

Ms. De Beer was tired, but she was determined to lift the dead weight as quickly and neatly as could be achieved. One end at a time seemed best, and so it was in this way that Me-Two's upper body rested on the blanket first, her lower parts following in quick-as-could-be-managed succession. The pulling of the upper parts, the shifting of the head and its nature, had pulled the roots of the whole arrangement out of the floorboards and they dangled thirstily from the neck of it all.

She grasped the top corners of the blanket and swept around in a gentle arc, turning Me-Two towards the door, and she began to walk ever so carefully back-wards. She stooped, dropping a corner for the briefest of moments, snatching the minutes that passed as well as her bag. The bag was nestled next to Me-Two to be pulled alongside; the minutes were filed away for a time where she might need an extra set of seconds, for when the firsts failed her.

The door was most pleased, completely and utterly delirious! She'd got it! And so quickly too, and without trying to do painful, prodding things to the room this time. She had got it, and she was the fastest yet to get it, and that was cause for an opening almost as grand as a closing.

As Ms. De Beer approached with her blanket-full of death and its accessories, the door opened wider than it needed to let her pass.

Chapter Eight

They passed, and then they were through, and the door shut quietly behind them. The night had gone, its last traces still lingered so it couldn't have been gone for long, but it was most definitely the morning. Ms. De Beer had not slept, not really, she had only tip-toed the line between sleep and wakefulness, not having fallen either way before the walls had started up their weak beat. She was tired, but it wasn't the thing. The thing was coming, she knew it, the real thing was on its way.

The real thing, the thing yet to be done, was very much already there, though she hadn't spotted it just yet. The thing, as it stood, again and in great detail, was the outside.

There had been a softening of Ms. De Beer as she'd passed through the house to the yard. It would have been a welcome change to her friends and family, had it not been too late to make amends with everyone she had lost in the wake of herself.

The step was impressed, as was the sad little window. The little window was so full of admiration at the thing almost having been done, and done so quickly it had to be said, that it cracked a bit at its middle. They had both been not a little upset that their time on the inside had been so fleeting, but there was something about the yard that was awfully nice, and they always seemed to forget that until they were back in it again. Besides, this wasn't the proper outside anyway, it just looked like it was, and while looks could be deceiving, they were something of a comfort to the window and the step.

The fence was much more solid than the walls had been, and Ms. De Beer felt herself relaxing along with her eyes and her grip. One could have spent all day in the other room trying to focus, but here in the yard the only shift was the occasional (manufactured but quite authentic) breeze tickling nature's curves into momentary straightness. She had dropped the corners of the blanket, staring out over the front yard with an air of triumph, until she had seen the bloody gate. There was a bloody gate! This was not quite out at all, this was still in.

She turned back door-wards, coming through as she had in a backwards manner, and was stooping just so to grasp the blanket again for one last 'pick a good spot and set up camp' sort of movement, when she spied the door and its boiling panels making light of her new focus. Just as the walls in the previous room had seethed across the joinery and swirled in a most unreal way, so too did the door's outside panels.

"I'm not spending all bloody day trying to focus on your silly door!" shouted Ms. De Beer. "There's a gate in front of me, so if you think I'm going to even think about that swirling thing then you're mad."

She wasn't sure who she was talking to, but she imagined that nature would deliver the message to wherever it needed to go. She wasn't sure how she was sure, but she was, and whatever it was giving her such faith in it all, well it had given her the right thing. Faith swept her words into the air, hitched them to the dust motes, sending a slight rustle of the leaves and trees to hurry it all along. The message had been sent, and things changed a little inside the things that had insides to share.

Being a proper little yard, with a proper little brick path and what would be a lovely rosy hedge when the time was right to bloom, there was a table sitting in the nicest spot for viewing the entire affair. Two chairs as well, but there was unlikely to be a need for two, what with Me-Two still being quite dead. The table and chairs were those adorable cast iron ones, all heavy and too hot in the sun, painted white and just the best looking set for such a setting, but they never were comfortable. There was sun, and it was quite hot. There was a glare on the chairs, and the table wasn't stable, so that when Ms. De Beer approached the area to put down her bag the whole thing wobbled at her a very bright opportunity to drop her things on the path. And she did.

She dropped her bag, and tripped over the leg of the brightest chair. The chair was awfully sorry about that, but it was the brightest, and so the best at obscuring direction when the sun rose at just that angle. It had only risen far enough to clear the fence, and while the chair was proud to be so bright, it did wonder if, in being so bright, it might be doing a disservice to other things that might have mattered a little bit.

She was tired, very tired indeed. She hadn't quite escaped, which was rather a disappointment. The fence was so high, and she was getting sick of it, just sick of almost-triumph and then none at all. She was closer now, she thought, but was she close enough? Close enough often missed, and wasn't a miss still a miss no matter how close you came?

The day, ignoring as it was the lack of a useful night for Ms. De Beer, was getting hotter and higher and fizzier than she could endure. The air crackled, each breeze drying and snapping as it passed her weary head, and she thought that perhaps some shade might be in order. Now was the time to wander the yard, to examine the garden closely and find a tree to sit under. Trees weren't as bright as tables, canopies more comfortable than chairs, so she strolled around the edges of the place looking for an even smaller place.

It wasn't the biggest of yards, but as children know there's always a place inside a place, a place that can't be seen unless you really look for it and choose to see it. There was always a spot under a bush, arching up and out to form a little house under the leaves, or maybe a tree with enough low branches and miraculous footholds to become a miniature house for hiding in. Ms. De Beer's brain wasn't so much curious as adamant that there should be something there, because the alternative didn't bear thinking about. If there were no shady hidey-holes to be found they were going to dry up in the sun, and while she was wet enough on the inside to deal with it for a time, she didn't think Me-Two and the vines connecting her head to her body would be able to stand the harsh rays for very long at all.

The step was bored, and watching the about-to-shatter window wasn't doing much for its spirits. It did, however, wonder just how long Ms. De Beer could withstand the heat of the day before she realised that blankets aren't just for keeping warm. The blanket itself was feeling rather put upon, and as such it still was, what with the corpse and the bag still weighing it down. Still, at least it was dead, the blanket didn't want to think about what would happen were the body to begin to sweat. Sweat always seemed to seep into fibres not accustomed to company, and it never really left even after it dried.

Despite much searching and channelling one's inner child, Ms. De Beer had not found a secret spot to hide from the sun's assault. She retreated to the white table set, wishing very much that it was a bit bigger, and taller, and perhaps didn't have quite so many gaps in its pretty metalworking. She knelt and shuffled her way under the table, noting that the bricks were a little cooler just there, but that she still couldn't turn her head in any direction that would stop the sun getting in her eyes. Sunglasses!

Three pairs of sunglasses, and they'd been there all the time, and for goodness sake what had she been thinking?

It was an inelegant dash, back up the path a few steps to the blanket and its cargo of death and useful things. Ms. De Beer rummaged in her bag for a pair of glasses, and while there were three in there, she knew there were, it took her longer than it should have.

Found at last, Ms. De Beer slipped on a pair of sunglasses and was very relieved indeed. She turned her head to the gate and took in its thin puzzle, scanned the fence for loose boards, and turned back in time to notice the edge of the blanket flapping gently in the breeze, revealing and concealing a small corner of shade with each breath.

The blanket again! She quietly congratulated herself for her foresight at having brought the blanket from the first room in the first place. Not luck, no, this was clearly her superior subconscious knowing just what would be required for the journey ahead, and though it wasn't a word, still wasn't a word, she knew that she was about to really shake off this state of movelessness.

The blanket made a very nice tent, when arranged with the chairs and the table. The white of the paint on the furniture proved to not be quite so white at all – it was actually very slightly blue. It wasn't quite so big either, any of it, once the blanket had settled and rustled over its frames. The set breathed out, and while it didn't shrink in an enormous way, it was enough to make it a little bit less roomy for Ms. De Beer, Me-Two's body, and the dust motes that had been trapped when the shade fell.

It was altogether too crowded by half, but Ms. De Beer hadn't noticed.

Before arranging the blanket over the top of the furniture, Ms. De Beer had arranged Me-Two across the chairs. She made a handy cross-beam, and Ms. De Beer was sure she wouldn't mind, being that she was out of the sun now too. Me-Two's hand hung down and brushed Ms. De Beer's shoulder, which would have been disconcerting under any other set of circumstances, but felt like an acknowledgement of a job well done to Ms. De Beer's tired mind. It had been a clever idea, it absolutely had.

She gazed up at the previous door, the one that continued to seethe when all around it did its best to be much realer than that, and she saw a small cupboard on the porch. Well, it wasn't a porch so much as a thin strip of ground and haphazard brickwork, skinny and damp but never touched by rain, choosing instead to suck up the moisture from the ground in a lazy slurp. There was some moss too, all puffy and praying for the slow, nightly creep of moisture to arrive earlier today.

Surely the tools with which to solve the gate weren't going to be so easy to come by! It felt calmer out here though, she had to admit that, and the pace seemed much less urgent than it had when she couldn't look up. Ms. De Beer reached up and pulled the corner of the blanket that had been obscuring Me-Two's face. She'd forgotten completely about the woman's desire to be looking up always, but now she had remembered, and perhaps that would be enough to counter all the rudeness she'd been obliged to indulge in up until this point.

And now there was the cupboard to consider. It was one of those little cupboards you could put just about anywhere – at the bedside, in the laundry, next to the arm of a sofa, or indeed out on a porch-not-porch. She would move it over to the blanket tent, perhaps, move it and give it a thorough examination.

And so the cupboard was dragged over to the tent, being that it was heavier than its size suggested, and Ms. De Beer rested for a moment before gently pulling the warped wood of its door towards her. This promised to be a cabinet of success, she was sure of it, and then she wasn't so sure of it at all. Inside the cupboard were only two things, neither of which seemed to be things that could be part of the bigger thing that needed doing.

Inside the cupboard were the following:

A large paintbrush, probably for painting houses.

A tin of blue paint, only obviously blue because some of its innards had been carelessly left to seep down the sides of the tin after its last use.

Of course it was blue. Naturally it would have to be a hue that connected itself in some way to the dead Me-Two, because she hadn't caused enough problems already, oh no, not even approaching enough! Ms. De Beer seethed and the door seethed back from the edge of the not-a-porch-really, and the air inside the tent grew as puffed as the moss and muggy. Ms. De Beer's circuits sparked inside her head, her eyes twitching and rolling.

This was a joke; it had to be a joke! Bloody blue! And what was she supposed to do with it? Ms. De Beer was at the end of her rope, and meant to tie up as many things as she could with it. She would bind them all and watch them push against their shackles, and she would laugh and laugh and laugh. But when the laughter had died she would still be there, and then what? Then she would have to untie it again.

There wasn't even anything that needed painting, at least not that she thought was looking decrepit enough in itself to subject it to a lick of blue. The fence was just the sort of rickety wooden thing that one wanted in a fence, and the side of the house that contained the door was just charming with its webs, and specks of paint missing here and there. But yes, then there was the door.

The door was not at all keen for a paint job, and it writhed across itself furiously at the very thought. Its panels swam and blistered with grey and not-as-grey, as if a stray storm cloud had somehow got itself attached to a frame and was trying its best to scud away. It tried to shrink, to bury itself further into the side of the house and encourage the worn weatherboards to extend themselves over to each other. It would open for no one now – that was a promise. That didn't matter though, because they were already through.

Ms. De Beer collected her limbs, and the paint, and approached the door. She could feel waves of something coming at her, not air she didn't think, but just as invisible whatever it was, and she had to work quite hard to push herself through the space until she arrived at the step. The step didn't like this one bit, but it couldn't see a way to stop whatever was about to happen. No one had ever tried to change the house before; no one had been brave enough to risk the ire of the doors. There would be a lot of slamming after this, and the step's top and bottom and sides, and whatever was inside them, would reverberate with it, it just knew it.

Paintbrush poised and tin of colour at the ready, Ms. De Beer set about opening the pot of paint. This proved trickier than she'd thought, and she had to remove her glasses and use them as a lever to prise the top from its bottom, which was hard to do when the glare of the day was in your eyes.

It was open now, and she dipped the brush into the fluid, pushing through a thin layer of oiliness to get to the sloppy pigment underneath. The oil puckered and filled the little chasm made by the brush's invasion, and she thought perhaps some stirring might be the thing. Not the thing, obviously, but a thing on the way to the thing, so important enough to be going on with.

The brush emerged, dripping blue tears if one were to be all melancholy about it, and Ms. De Beer began to apply herself to her work. Long, wet strokes of the brush slid down the door, the blue shimmering for a moment before turning a rather vulgar shade of purple – the purple of unsullied veins, the purple of a plum so ripe and juicy that it would stain your chin for a few days and have you looking like a vampire in the process. You could never wash that sort of purple off fast enough, it always lingered. It was the colour of the inside of her, though Ms. De Beer couldn't have known that.

It didn't take long to finish the first coat, although she'd had to jump to reach the uppermost corners of the panels. There was not a speck left unpainted now, and she was sweaty with the effort. The blanket eyed her sweatiness warily, its linty, bobbly parts turning and opening in the style of the eyes of newborn kittens, all gluey and milky with newness.

She stood back, as one does after they've done something they're proud of without an audience, and surveyed the streaky handiwork of the first coat. The door's seething was mostly obscured now, but not quite enough for it to be unnoticeable out of the corner of one's eye.

Quite a few dust motes, having escaped from under the blanket, had been far too curious for their own good, becoming stuck in the thin paint between streaks. The more that came, the grittier the paint began to look. It would definitely need another coat, at least that's what the step thought, annoyed as it was by the blue droplets that had landed atop its top during the first coat and not looking forward to more. The sad little window had a smudge of blue of its own too, and it ran across the crack in its middle, a sky coloured bandage.

"You missed a bit."

Chapter Nine

Ms. De Beer jumped and twitched and spun to the voice behind her. Me-Two stood wonkily in the growing heat of the day, still blue-ish in the face, but decidedly green in other places. She held gingerly onto one of the white chairs, each curled finger topped with a tiny leafy sprout, baby vines that sprang from the fingertips like a manicure gone wild. Bigger vines encircled her neck and hung in a mane onto her shoulders, small bugs squirming their way through the leaves and wondering why their home had just become so very upright.

Ms. De Beer's pointy arse hit the ground before she'd even known she was losing her knees. There were very few moments in which Ms. De Beer could not be counted on to have something to say on whatever the matter might be, and this was one. The sparks in her brain subsided, humming to themselves while they waited for her to regain control of her senses and say something flint-blunt to set them off again.

They would be waiting for some time.

Ms. De Beer remained on the ground for some minutes, all attempts to reconcile the sudden combination of nature and the dead woman rather weak and feeble. When she finally did speak, it was not blunt, or witty, or clever.

"Ah, well, you're back. That's fortunate, I was about to get that gate open for us." She stammered with memory, all the little indignities she'd wrought on Me-Two's lifeless form taking much greater shape now that it wasn't quite so lifeless anymore. Would she remember? Perhaps there would be a gap in proceedings for her. Ms. De Beer could only hope.

"I really am awfully grateful that you brought me through with you, that was very kind, goodness knows I could have been lying half in and half out of this place forever," Me-Two said. "Now, I think I've rested long enough, perhaps I could help?"

She didn't wait for a response, picking up the paint tin and the brush and heading towards the gate.

"This really is rather an unusual colour, I don't know that I've ever seen it before," she said, and then it hit her, not quite as hard as the first door had, but certainly it made its mark. "Is... Is this blue?"

Ms. De Beer nodded, which arrived as more of a wobble of the neck than a nod of the head.

"Blue! I can see it! This is wonderful!" Me-Two's happy shrieking filled the yard with noise, shifted the rays of light, and echoed off the fence, coming back to her to be used again later. The happy noises hadn't been out for a long time, and they weren't missing the chance to hurry back to her to be used again.

Such was her glee that Me-Two dipped her leafy fingers into the paint, watching the ribbons of goo-blue run back to the tin. She did it over and over, blue ridges forming under her fingernails. Each plunge into the blue was deeper and deeper, and her whole hand was syrupy-slick with it before long. And before long, she had made blue hand prints all over the tall, thin gate, connecting them with little smears and daubs of colour until the whole thing resembled a spider web, or the sky through a latticed screen.

The fresh paint shone in the light, dappled itself, but also sent dapples out and around the edges of Ms. De Beer's sunglasses, tiptoeing over her lashes and settling somewhere unreachable in the corners of her eyes. As was customary by now, the gate creaked in welcome, and Me-Two, while knowing she was on the right track, was more than a little bit cautious. It would not do to lose her head twice.

"I'm feeling a bit tired, do you think you could take over?" she enquired, making excuses, although Ms. De Beer was still in such a state of shock that she wouldn't have noticed anyway.

Ms. De Beer nodded again, this time in the conventional way, and rose to her feet. She took the paintbrush from the grass next to Me-Two's feet and began to fill in the gaps, swirling the brush, not wanting to miss a bit this time. There was no transformation to purple, just the dusty blue hue and a predictable outcome – the gate was almost completely blue, and was getting bluer.

Ms. De Beer had heard the creak too, and while she knew it was a sign of an opening to come, she too was hesitant to wedge anything through until the thing had opened wide enough for living things to pass through without fear of a slam. As it was, this would be a 'keep your arms close and avoid sticking your neck out' sort of a situation, she was sure of that.

The paint was drying quickly in the glare of the day. As there had been a creak, Ms. De Beer thought perhaps she could try something she hadn't thought of until now – she could just try to open the bloody thing like a normal door, and without doubt. Brain sparks returned, and she stepped back briefly before stepping forward again in a sedate run-up to try the gate. It didn't budge, which the fence had known the whole time, and would have mentioned if it had been asked, but it hadn't, so it continued to keep the outside of outside on the outside.

"I am getting very sick of doors and gates," Ms. De Beer moaned.

Over at the table setting Me-Two was feeling no bolder than before, however where Ms. De Beer had sparks she had seedlings and shoots. A slight wiggle at the fingertip, and a shoot did what the name suggests, snaking from Me-Two's finger and crawling from the tabletop to the ground. As it grew towards the gate new leaves appeared on its length, and new roots too, tethering it as it passed, grounding it so as to let it move on.

It kept shooting until it reached the edge of the gate, and it didn't stop there. It didn't go forward either – the vine-y finger doubled back, snagging itself on a gate board and heading back towards its hand. The gate came with it for a time, scraping the grass beneath it into green-bloody stumps, white at the core and leeching life into the lawn

The gate was open, not entirely, but open enough to go through without having to suck in one's stomach and hope for the best. This would require only the hope, and both of the woman, the red and the blue, took their time in collecting themselves for departure. Ms. De Beer picked up her bag, inside which was Me-Two's bag. She removed the smaller from the larger, and handed the smaller bag to Me-Two, who was quite pleased that it had come through too.

Before they could pass through the gate, there was the matter of uprooting Me-Two's vine from the grass and between the pavers. Ms. De Beer moved in front of Me-Two, gently pulling up each tiny root-anchor as she edged toward the gate. Me-Two followed her, taking two small steps for each root that was loosened and released. She coiled the vine in her hand as they crept forward, looping it gently around her wrist, the extension of herself bangle-d neatly and safe from harm.

They reached the gate, Ms. De Beer stooping to unhook the curve of the vine from the bottom of its boards. Once released, it was only a gentle tug and the rest of the vine was dangling from Me-Two's wrist, daintily oozing the perfume of fresh earth and new growth into the air around them. Another three steps and both of her, both of them, were through the gate, and there was no more outside on that side.

It was a stroke of genius, as the sad little window saw it, pure cleverness wrapped up in chlorophyll. It swelled with pride in these strange people, and as it swelled it began to crack further, and further, and then the frame couldn't contain it any longer. The sad little window burst into hundreds of glittering shards, fluttering as much as glass can, then nestling into the grass and bricks, a few wayward sparkles landing on the step.

It didn't hurt, not really, but it felt very odd indeed, and each piece of the little window was in danger of becoming sadder than it had been as a whole. They hadn't known, though, that the gate was letting in even more light than before now that it was open, and that there was more here to catch than there had ever been. Light swept over to the pieces, propositioned them wildly and without fear, and they danced each other through the air. It was light in embrace, and it looked a lot like the surface of the glittering sea would to a drowning man, slowly sinking under the mosaic, unable to get back but appreciative of the view.

One tiny shard, catching and whirling as much light as its miniscule facets could manage, did wonder for a moment if they would melt under the glare and heat of all the attention. It needn't have worried – the harsh heat was reflected back to the door, magnified, bubbling the paint and eventually beginning to blacken the mottled wood beneath. With no one there to put out the fire, it not only started but also continued, and there was more than enough light for everyone.

Chapter Ten

This was most definitely not outside. Ms. De Beer took in the white walls and the eye chart and the small table with all the leaflets, and she cursed this room. This useless, charmless, heartbreaking room was the doctor's room, and she wanted to be out of it more than she had all of the other rooms combined. This room was full of judgement and things she couldn't do, and she knew that it wouldn't be making allowances for her.

Me-Two looked perturbed herself, having never been fond of medical facilities in any of their forms. They always seemed to want to fix things that couldn't be fixed, or at least make them look as though they weren't broken, and that seemed an awful shame.

After a few minutes loitering nervously by the door, which was no longer a gate, they put down their belongings and dared to sit on the nasty old chairs that were arranged conspiratorially next to the doctor's desk. The doctor's chair was rather new and comfortable looking by comparison, but neither of them wanted to risk inviting the doctor to suddenly appear and evict them from its faux-leather clutches.

Ms. De Beer was not at all comfortable in this space, not one bit. She looked around desperately for a clue, for something that would nudge the welcoming creak of an almost-got-it to appear, but this room was the most normal of places she had been so far on this journey. She hated to use the word 'journey', it seemed too much like a brash ballad crossed with a sense of dumb pride, but she supposed you could liken those things to what had happened, at a push.

There were filing cabinets of varying sizes and colours arranged in a bank to the side of the doctor's desk, little skyscrapers filled with little lives. Very inefficient to keep paper files, Ms. De Beer thought, and altogether too prone to prying eyes. She knew this because she had opened the drawer that corresponded to her surname, and was quietly sorting through, looking for her file.

Ah, here it was. Ms. M. T. De Beer – 34 years of age, less-than-average height, mostly-average weight (with a bit to come and go on), and chronic heart trauma, exacerbated by her unwillingness to see what she is doing to herself. Ms. De Beer paused here, anger growing in her gut, reality trying desperately to get in and tamp it back down to a slow burn rather than an inferno. Reality smudged from the ink of the file, coated her fingertips, exposed the ridges and whorls of them, and made them more her than they had been before. It tried to soak into her pores, and they resisted for a while. It was a slow battle, right up until the paper cut and the tears.

Indeed, Ms. De Beer had cut herself on the very real edge of the file, a small cut, nothing to be worried about in the scheme of things, and there was a blurry ooze from it that swirled across the print as she ran her finger along the lines. Each line was underlined with it, the words moving on the page as they struggled to stay in formation. The mini-sting of it, as there always is with a paper cut, travelled from her finger to her eyes, inviting the first leap of tears to creep from between her lashes, testing the water as if they weren't already the water themselves.

Several of the bolder tears banded together, having been waiting some time for the thing that would break the dam, and they ran together, quickly and only leaving a trace of themselves behind, down Ms. De Beer's cheek to her proud chin. Her chin wasn't feeling quite as proud as it normally would have, and it did nothing as the group of tears flung themselves off Ms. De Beer and on to the page. Now they could mingle! They mingled with the ink, mostly, making tiny cloudy puddles of themselves in the process. Gravity got in on it too, stamped its authority on the small wonders, and it tipped the inky tears finger-wards, towards the paper cut.

That was how the truth got in. Once it was in it circulated, passing many stations until it got to its stop. Off at the brain, and then a short hop to the eyes. Very efficient system – no traffic, always moving steadily – but then it always was, and even if it missed its stop, there was always another line to catch, and the red and white cells were a pleasant bunch to travel with, if a bit hurried and hyper-vigilant. Still, they had good reason to be – they were losing their own at an alarming rate.

Me-Two, having taken in every corner and crevice of the room so as not to miss some crafty, concealed GP who would fix her into submission, turned to Ms. De Beer to make a suggestion. She had not expected the bright red bloom on the front of Ms. De Beer's shirt, nor had she expected it to be running to the floor in a little, wet marathon, and it was then that she gasped and pointed.

"What?" Ms. De Beer was growing more irritated by the moment, regaining her former disdain for the daftness of her silly twin, almost forgetting that mere hours ago her doppelgänger had been cold under a blanket.

"Your chest, and the floor... Oh, you're bleeding!"

Ms. De Beer was bleeding, just as the doctor had pointed out all those days, or possibly weeks ago, and when she looked down she saw the wetness of her shirt, and the creep of the blood as it seeped towards the floor. She saw it; the mysterious red of her heart that was leaking itself away, slowly but with intent. With each heaving breath, the fabric of her shirt bubbled, slick red spheres of life popping as they gave up their air, and she wondered why she hadn't seen it before, why it hadn't blurred her to herself as it did everything else.

She could see it now, the red of it all, but she didn't lose her knees this time – they were in on it, it seemed, locked in place to help further the illusion that everything was quite alright, and that she hadn't been letting herself bleed to death for quite some time.

She supposed she should try to stop it somehow. They were, after all, in a doctor's office, and there would be something here that could stem the flow, surely. A first aid kit on the wall beckoned, brightening perceptibly so as to be noticed by the stricken woman and her flighty friend. Me-Two did notice it, and rather uncharacteristically for her, she ripped it off the wall, losing two of her finger-leaves in the process.

"There must be something in here. Oh gosh, it's quite a lot of blood, how did you not notice it?"

Ms. De Beer did not have an answer to that question, so she stayed silent, choosing to slow the beat of her traitorous heart, rather than speed its weeping with her anger.

There was nothing of use in the kit, or so Me-Two thought, nothing that could be relied upon to worm its way into the fleshy highways of Ms. De Beer and go to work repairing the rend. Scared, and unsure what to do next, Me-Two turned her face to Ms. De Beer, just in time to see her swallowing a needle and thread.

"I don't know that that's the best way to fix it," said Me-Two, wondering (and not for the first time) whether Ms. De Beer was actually a bit mad at her core.

Ms. De Beer wasn't entirely sure what had made her swallow the needle. She had found it very irksome to look at it, in all its useful, practical glory, and know that it couldn't be properly applied to fix whatever it was that had torn inside her. It seemed to mock her, and so she decided to make it go away, to consume it and absorb some of that useful essence as it went down.

It went down fairly smoothly, all things considered, not sticking into anything until it reached Ms. De Beer's stomach and became snagged on wet, hungry walls. It wasn't stuck for long, unpicking a tiny tear in the lining with which to continue its journey heart-wards. It didn't bother her anyway, and she wasn't exactly looking for ways to be happy. Swallowing sharp, metal things wasn't on the list of things that could make you happy, as least as far as she knew, but it might make its debut appearance if it worked.

The room wasn't quite as alive as the others had been. It was soulless and dim at the corners, and there were shadows that sat lazily on just about everything. The laziness washed over everything, even the urgency, and it was because of this that Me-Two and Ms. De Beer had not noticed the door. The door out of this room was frosted glass, shining and dull all at once if that were possible. This door, unlike the others, did not have a lock, or a snib, or anything to keep it in its place, and it wobbled slightly when either of the woman moved through the fuggy air of the room.

Me-Two was much more concerned with all the blood than the door, wanting with all her good self to find herself a bit more sensible. She would have liked to know what to do to stem it, to alleviate Ms. De Beer's pain, although she didn't seem to be feeling any, at least not in an obvious way. Ms. De Beer just sat quietly, papers in hand and looking worse for wear, and stared at the eye chart on the wall.

Me-Two followed her lead, sitting in one of the lumpy chairs and gazing at the leaflets on the table. They spent a long time not doing anything, both lost in thought as to how they would open the door, but one was more lost than the other. Ms. De Beer was not even sure she wanted to get out anymore.

Hours passed like this, hours in which the light didn't change to show its passing. The hours could have been minutes, and the actual minutes Ms. De Beer had up her sleeve came out to make friends with their fellow gauges of time. The air prickled with their passage, and Me-Two felt all out of sorts, a bit jittery, perhaps in need of a quick jog-on-the-spot or a few laps of the roo.

She rose from her seat, wobble-legged and bowed at the brain, and set off for her short circuit around the drabness of the walls. She started at the desk where the chairs were, took the steps required to meet the corner, turned, and strode the faded carpet to the next corner, not bothering to stop and see the sights. She'd seen it all as they came through the door into the room, seen the eye chart and the leaflets and the dusty filing cabinets, she'd even seen the lungs on the table, a plastic model of something that really shouldn't be that still. It was unnerving.

She turned at the next corner, avoided the half-dead potted fern and turned again when she saw the door properly. They'd not really looked at it, not really, and she hovered a polite distance away, hoping for a creak. Did glass doors creak? Probably not, but there could be a noise of some kind, so getting a tiny bit closer seemed the best course of action.

Me-Two took two steps closer to the door, and there was indeed a noise. There was a sound that put her in mind of a blade slashing paper, a whoosh of cutting air, and the door opened. It was automatic. She stepped back, and the door closed, stepped forward and it opened once more. This was just the best thing that could possibly have happened!

"We just had to look at it a bit closer!" she squealed, hopping from foot to foot and clapping her hands, rapidly and without much of a noise at all. "Look! It's open!"

Ms. De Beer looked, and the door was indeed open. She didn't, however, want to go through it. She breathed out as hard as she could, hoping to expel the truth she'd taken in, to send its spores out and away so they could grow in the damp innards of someone else's life. With each inward breath the needle, having found the tiniest of heart-holes to plug, poked out painfully from her chest, making a tent of her skin, white and thin at its peak, ropey ridges stretching out and over her bruised ribs before settling back down to wait for the next pitching of breath.

She did not want to go through.

In the end...

Me-Two tried all the well-worn techniques she could think of to entice Ms. De Beer through the door.

"This will be the last one, I should think," she said, almost chirruping with it, overly twinkly and wild-eyed with impatience. "Come on now, it'd be an awful shame to get this far and end up in here forever."

Ms. De Beer remained as stony-faced as she had been for the previous hours, staring at the new and rather alarming line of red letters on the eye chart that she had consistently missed on previous visits. That was, of course, when she wasn't watching the fruit bowl on the doctor's desk. It had been full of lemons, which she'd found quite absurd, but was now full of oranges.

"What if the doctor comes back?"

Ms. De Beer flinched at the idea, curled up as if she was on fire, and looked at the door despairingly. What if the doctor came back? What would she do if he came back and told her that he'd told her so, that she should do something about things, that he could fix her? What would he do about the thing, the bleeding and the pain she'd only just noticed? Did he know what the thing really was? She would have to come back here eventually, that much was clear, and the wound would need tending to, but she really couldn't cope with it now. Now, all of a sudden, she wanted to go home.

She stood, and she picked up her bag, and she shuffled over to where Me-Two was standing by the door. Me-Two took Ms. De Beer by the elbow, ever so gently, ready to steer if need be. It was in this way that the bleeding woman and her once dead friend-enhanced-by-nature slowly moved through the door.

The door made its whooshing noise as it opened, and another once they were through, and it was very dark then, neither woman sure if they had their eyes open or closed. They stopped, and waited, and felt as though they had been swallowed by something that was sleeping.

Late! The sun had not been expecting to be called upon so soon, and it went up in the way that curtains do at the theatre, or eyelids do at the end of a particularly unpleasant nightmare – all at once, yet with resolve and a measured pace. It all grew clearer, and then not so clear with all the light in eyes and the glare of the day they had walked into. Ms. De Beer fumbled in her bag for sun-glasses, handing Me-Two a pair as she hastily slipped a pair on herself, getting the arm of them in her ear before she finally found shady relief.

"I live here," said Ms. De Beer.

They had indeed arrived at Ms. De Beer's house, in Stanley Street, with the roses and the weatherboards and the little windows that chattered to each other with the rising of the sun. The roses were stubbornly refusing to bloom, although one small bud had taken pity on Ms. De Beer, leaving a sliver of petal to protrude from its little green hand. But still, there was the front porch, the old, rickety chair that sat unused under the doorbell, and there was the old, gnarled orange tree. The orange tree was usually in the back yard, but eager to finally be picked it had made its way to the front, so heavy with fruit that really if they didn't harvest something, finally pull an orb from among the leaves, it might just have to die, or give in to the wriggling fruit fly maggots that were eating it down to the seeds.

Ms. De Beer and Me-Two walked cautiously up the path to the step, which wasn't as chatty as previous steps had been, each feeling the gravity of the situation for different reasons. Gravity wasn't really interested in reasons, it just knew that you had to go where you had to go, and so the tilt was the same for both of them, slightly downward before the upward.

They stood at the door, and it was rather inexplicably red. Ms. De Beer's door had not been red before, and the paint looked as though it were still wet. She pressed a finger to it, setting the grooves of her fingerprint into the greasy surface. Ms. De Beer wondered where she should wipe the paint from her finger, and then chose the already bloody front of her shirt on which to remove the stain. It came away redder than before.

Ah, no matter, it would all come out in the wash.

Me-Two's vines crept up the posts and eaves of the porch, winding themselves into their new home as if they had been there always, and who was to say they hadn't? Spiders and beetles jostled for position in the lovely new foliage, and it all got a bit lusher than it had been before. Just a bit mind you, it takes time to put down proper roots and establish one's self.

A hand with a red-smudged finger and a hand with leafy fingertips reached for the doorknob, almost movelessly, if that were a word, going under and over each other as they twisted and pushed. The door opened, and one Ms. M. T. De Beer, of 37 Stanley Street, stepped inside.

Author's Note

Pre-diagnosis, I assimilated well into society, it has to be said – on the outside at least – learning how to mimic acceptable neuro-typical behaviour and opinion until it became hard to distinguish the learnt from the felt. I'm still in the process of weeding out and unlearning the things that keep me from being myself.

In the past I took a "person with autism" approach, not really understanding what that meant and how it wouldn't work in the scheme of things. "Person with autism" suggests that I have something, an affliction, some kind of defect or disease.

Me and It.

I am a person, that much is true, but I'm also a variation, an autistic person. Autism is not an unfortunate add-on to a separate entity. It is me.

I'm not ill. I have a difference in the wiring of my brain, and if you could hand me a pill and say, "Look, we found a cure!", I would certainly not be lining up with a glass of water and out-stretched hand. It's my neurology, and that means it touches everything I think, or do, or feel.

I'm autistic first, at least to my mind (and my mind is autistic, so I guess it would tell me that, knowing itself the best and all). It saddens me more than I can express that I not only inwardly subscribed to the affliction model, but that I outwardly expressed it, and to people who were trying to tell me something. I wasn't listening, to them or myself.

There is a growing community of autistic people trying to get the world to listen, with their own ideas around support services, respectful language, and the lack of real discourse on these and many other issues – discourse that actually listens to and involves autistic people.

We have something to add to the conversation, and every right to add it.

This is an edited excerpt from an article originally published in The Big Smoke, *titled 'Autism does speak – Will we listen?'*

Acknowledgements

For Mad Dog – You have always reminded me who I am, where I come from, and that I can do the thing, whatever the thing may be. Thank you, Dad-among-dads.

For R & C – You are the best creations I could imagine, and you both fill me with such hope. Thank you for your faith in me, and for filling my days with all the good things.

For Steve – You put up with me while I wrote this, and so many other things. You read them, sometimes when it was the last thing you felt like doing, and you told me I shouldn't stop. Thank you, bestie. X

For Andon – Every tiny piece of this, as it came, you read it, and you were honest. You helped me see. Oldest friend, I am grateful.

Sarah Madden

Sarah Madden is an autistic writer, originally from New Zealand. After four years living in the Middle East, she moved to Victoria where she has been based for the past five years.

Since landing in Australia, Madden has rediscovered her love of writing and words, and was awarded a Write-ability Fellowship by Writers Victoria in 2014. Madden writes fiction, memoir and poetry, most with a lyrical, slightly magical treatment woven through the threads of the everyday. Madden has been published, as Sarah Widdup, by *Underground Writers*, *The Big Smoke* and *Hot Chicks with Big Brains.*

www.ingramcontent.com/pod-product-compliance
Lightning Source LLC
Chambersburg PA
CBHW051955290426
44110CB00015B/2249
* 9 7 8 0 6 4 8 1 7 4 2 3 3 *